PREFACE

What is a **niche**?

A niche is a specialism that caters to a certain market or group of people.

If we relate this to business the oxford dictionary definition is as follows "A specialized segment of the market for a particular kind of product or service."

Finding a profitable niche that can actually increase the conversion rate is of utmost importance for small businesses to reach their customers.

Keeping in mind the competition factor in today's digital world a specific targeted micro-niche-oriented blog/affiliate site/e-commerce site can rank faster as compared to a multi-niche site.

So, choose your niche wisely specifically focussing on profit rate and your targeted customer needs.

Small businesses or newly created blogs immensely in need of a great niche or micro-niche ideas that can really help them to reach their audience.

Here you will find 1000+ broad niche, sub-niche & micro-niche ideas.

Hopefully, you will find this book helpful regarding your needs.

Thanks & Regards

Rajdeep Dey

By analyzing various aspects on blogging and a after doing thorough research on several needs which people generally search on internet I personally lists down **almost 1000 odd niches, sub-niche and micro-niches ideas** which you can apply on your personal or affiliate marketing blogs.

These niche ideas helped many people to deal with their confusion to select their topic of blogging and eventually helped them to become great entrepreneur in respective fields.

I have listed down below the main broad topics along with their niches & micro-niches ideas. Hopefully this list will help you to **become a great entrepreneur and motivate to start your own blog**.

1. Acne and Skin Care
2. Alcohol
3. Art
4. Baby and Maternity
5. Blockchain and Cryptocurrency
6. Books and Fiction
7. Business and Career
8. Cameras and Photography
9. Cars and Vehicles
10. Cooking and Recipes
11. Crafts and DIY
12. Diet and Weight Loss
13. Digital Marketing and MMO
14. Exercise
15. Farming

16.   Fashion
17.   Fishing
18.   Gardening and Lawn Care
19.   Health
20.   Makeup and Beauty
21.   Martial Arts
22.   Music and Instruments
23.   Outdoors
24.   Pets and animal care
25.   Sports
26.   Technology and Gadgets
27.   Travel
28.   Wedding

1. Acne and Skin Care

Acne and skin care is a topic that's very close to the heart of a lot of people. Since it's a real problem in the facial beauty, there's a large potential for many skin care related niches.

- • Acne Allergies
- • Acne Cream
- • Acne No More
- • Acne Scars
- • Acne Treatments
- • Adult Acne
- • Anti Aging
- • Anti Aging Foods
- • Baby Lotion
- • Bath Lotion
- • Birthmarks
- • Body Lotion
- • Cellulite Remedies
- • Cellulite Removal

- • Foot Care
- • Hand Lotion
- • Natural Skin Care
- • Natural Wrinkle Treatment
- • Scars
- • Skin Care
- • Skin Care Routine
- • Soap for Dry Skin
- • Soap For Sensitive Skin
- • Stretch Marks
- • Teenage Acne
- • Younger Skin

2. Alcohol

From home brewing to monthly tasting packages of beer, wine, and whiskey, alcohol is an industry with decent niche potential for the right marketer.

- • Bar Supplies
- • Beer Making
- • Beer Of The Month Club
- • Beercations
- • Cocktail Recipes
- • Clubbing on a Budget
- • Craft Beer
- • Gin Lovers
- • Home Bars
- • Home brewing
- • Home Brewing Supplies
- • How to Cure Hangovers
- • How to Make Cocktails
- • Making Wine
- • Rum Lovers

- • Run A Bar
- • Wine Making
- • Wine Of The Month Club
- • Wine Tasting

3. Art

From selling your own paintings to collecting historical art to teaching beginners, art has a lot of valid niches. Use one of the choices below to start a website and online business.

- • Art Collecting
- • Art History
- • Art Investing
- • Art Supplies
- • Azulejo
- • Bodyart
- • Cartoonist
- • Fabric Painting
- • Fine Art
- • How To Make Rock Sculptures
- • Illustration
- • Learn Sand Art
- • Learn Snow Sculpting
- • Learn To Draw
- • Manga Tutorials
- • Mail Art
- • Metalwork
- • Mosaics
- • Paintings
- • Performing Arts
- • Sculptures
- • Visual Arts
- • Wall Art

- • Wall Hangings
- • Watercolor Art

4. Baby and Maternity

Baby products is a booming industry, as there is nothing a parent is more passionate about than their expected (or existing) infant.

- • Adopting A Baby
- • Adoption
- • Baby Accessories
- • Baby Bathing
- • Baby Car Seats
- • Baby Care
- • Baby Development
- • Baby Feeding
- • Baby Gear
- • Baby Gifts
- • Baby Music
- • Baby Nursery
- • Baby Shower
- • Babysitting Service
- • Baby Sleep
- • Baby Strollers
- • Bed Wetting
- • Birth
- • Birth Announcement
- • Breastfeeding Help
- • Breastfeeding Diet
- • Daycare
- • Dealing with Allergies
- • Dealing with Miscarriage
- • Dealing with Twins
- • Maternity

- •   • Maternity Clothing
- •   • Potty Training
- •   • Pregnancy
- •   • Pregnancy Diet
- •   • Pregnancy Massage
- •   • Pregnancy Nutrition
- •   • Prenatal Vitamins
- •   • Stop Bedwetting

5. Blockchain and Cryptocurrency

Bitcoin and other cryptocurrencies have proven they're here to stay, with a **whopping $8.8 trillion** traded in spot and futures markets in Q1 2020. The **price of bitcoin hit a record high of over $41,000** on first week of January, 2021 and has a **market value of over $700 billion** and thus pushed the value of entire cryptocurrency market to surpass $1 trillion for the 1st time.

- •   • Binance Coin
- •   • BitCoin
- •   • BitCoin Tutorials
- •   • Blockchain Tutorials
- •   • Blockchain Developer
- •   • Cryptocoin Mining
- •   • Cryptocurrency
- •   • Cryptocurrency Rates
- •   • Cryptocurrency Rankings
- •   • Dash Coin
- •   • Ethereum Coin
- •   • EOS

- • Libra
- • Litecoin
- • Litecoin Coin
- • Ripple Coin
- • Tether Coin
- • Zcash Coin

6. Books and Fiction

Both as a writer, book reviewer, and writing coach, there are many categories, and inevitably, niches in the book market.

- • Adventure
- • Altered Books
- • Biography
- • Book Author
- • Book Of The Month Club
- • Bookbinding
- • Coloring Books for Adults
- • Comic Books
- • Comics
- • Essays
- • Fantasy
- • Fiction
- • Mystery
- • Novel
- • Nonfiction
- • Pop-Up Books
- • Publish Your Own Book
- • Sci-Fi
- • Thriller
- • Script Writing
- • Speed Reading
- • Book Excerpts

- • Reading Apps
- • Writing Poetry
- • Literature
- • Love Poetry
- • Love Quotes
- • How to Write Faster
- • Audio Books
- • Voicing Audio Books

7. Business and Career

As the primary source of income for most people, this is a topic many are passionate about. Millions of people are looking for tips on running a successful business or architecting a great career.

- • Business Ideas
- • Business Loans
- • Business Start Up
- • Career Planning
- • College Scholarships
- • Consulting
- • Copywriting
- • CV
- • CV Writing
- • CV Writing Service
- • Data Entry
- • Economic Recession
- • Entrepreneurship Development
- • Find A Job
- • Interview FAQ
- • Job Interviews
- • Job Interview Tips
- • Job Interview Training

- • Job Skill
- • Leadership Development
- • Negotiating a raise
- • Online Degree
- • Online Jobs
- • Outsourcing
- • Raise Negotiation
- • Resume
- • Resume Writing
- • Resume Writing Service
- • Resume Writing Tips
- • Retirement
- • Retirement Planning
- • Sales Skills
- • Sales Tips
- • Small Business Advice
- • Small Business Grants
- • Social Networking
- • Software Developer
- • Start a Business
- • Start a Radio Show
- • Starting a Brand
- • Starting a Business
- • Startup
- • Tax Help
- • Unemployment
- • Wealthy
- • Working for Startups
- • Workplace Motivation
- • Write a Cover Letter (CV)

8. Cameras, Photography and Videography

Cameras and photography are huge passions for a lot of people, from hobbyists to full-time professionals. With tons of people looking to increase their skill and buy the best gear, this category has plenty of niches to choose from.

- • 360 Cameras
- • Compact Digital Cameras
- • Digital SLR Cameras
- • Mirrorless Cameras
- • Action Cameras
- • Film Cameras
- • Point-and-shoot Cameras
- • Beginner Cameras
- • Photography
- • Abstract Photography
- • Adventure Photography
- • Architectural Photography
- • Astrophotography
- • Black and White Photography
- • Business Photography
- • Candid Photography
- • Cityscape Photography
- • Commercial Photography
- • Composite Photography
- • Creative Photography
- • Documentary Photography
- • Drone Photography
- • Double-exposure Photography
- • Editorial Photography
- • Event Photography
- • Family Photography
- • Fashion Photography
- • Film Photography

- • Fine Art Photography
- • Food Photography
- • Golden Hour Photography
- • Holiday Photography
- • Indoor Photography
- • Infrared Photography
- • Landscape Photography
- • Lifestyle Photography
- • Long Exposure Photography
- • Macro Photography
- • Milky Way Photography
- • Minimalist Photography
- • Newborn Photography
- • Night Photography
- • Pet Photography
- • Photojournalism
- • Portrait Photography
- • Product Photography
- • Real Estate Photography
- • Seascape Photography
- • Social Media Photography
- • Sports Photography
- • Still-life Photography
- • Surreal Photography
- • Street Photography
- • Time-lapse Photography
- • Travel Photography
- • Underwater Photography
- • Urban Exploration Photography
- • War Photography
- • Wedding Photography
- • Wildlife Photography
- • Time-lapse Videos
- • Tutorial Videos

- • Video Interviews
- • Promotional Videos
- • Slow-mo Videos
- • Ultra High-speed Cameras
- • Filmmaking
- • Photo Editing
- • Photoshop
- • Photoshop Tutorials
- • Smartphone Photography
- • Video Editor
- • Video Producer

9. Cars and Vehicles

There is a considerable number of consumers who are emotionally attached to their cars. That means there are many viable niches in car sales, service, customization, and accessories.

- • Auto Repair At Home
- • Automobile Subwoofers
- • Best Used Cars
- • Box Trucks
- • Buy Tires
- • Buying A Used Car
- • Car Accessories
- • Car Auctions
- • Car Batteries
- • Car Chargers
- • Car Charging services
- • Car Cleaning
- • Car Customizing
- • Car Dealing
- • Car Electronics
- • Car Maintenance

14

- • Car Paint
- • Car Parts Online
- • Car Repair
- • Car Subwoofer
- • Car Window Tinting
- • Cargo Van
- • Certified Pre-Owned
- • Convertible
- • Coupe
- • Crossover
- • Custom car
- • Diesel
- • Electric Car Battery
- • Electric Car Charger
- • Go Kart Plans
- • Go Kart Racing
- • Go Karts
- • Hatchbacks
- • Hybrid/Electric
- • Ice Cream Trucks
- • Learn Driving Theory
- • Learn How to Drive
- • Lease Deals
- • Limousines
- • Luxury Cars
- • Passenger Buses
- • Passenger Vehicles
- • Pickup Trucks
- • RV Accessories
- • RV Parts
- • RV Travel
- • Saving on Fuel
- • Scooters
- • Sedans

- • Sport Utility Vehicles (SUVs)
- • Sports Car
- • Trucks
- • Truck Accessories
- • Used Car Loans
- • Vans
- • Vintage Car Restoration
- • Vintage Cars

10. Cooking and Recipes

Food isn't only a necessity for survival, it's also a reliable source of pleasure for many. As a result, there are hundreds of niches within cooking and food, including baking, pastry, smoothies, and more.

- • 5 Star Restaurant Recipes
- • Anabolic Cooking
- • Asian Cooking
- • Bacon Of The Month Club
- • Baking
- • Baking Parchment
- • Baking Sheet
- • Baking Supplies
- • Balloon Whisk
- • Barbecues
- • BBQ Recipes
- • BBQing
- • Beef
- • Beef Recipes
- • Binge Eating
- • Blender
- • Bottle Opener
- • Bread Baking

- • Bread Bin
- • Bread Knife
- • Bread Recipes
- • Breadmakers
- • Breakfast Recipes
- • British Recipes
- • Cake Decorating
- • Cake Decorating Supplies
- • Can Opener
- • Casserole
- • Catering
- • Catering Supplies
- • Cheese Making
- • Cheese Of The Month Club
- • Chef's Knives
- • Chicken
- • Chicken Recipes
- • Chinese Recipes
- • Chocolate Recipes
- • Chopping/Cutting Board(s)
- • Coffee
- • Coffee Lovers
- • Coffee Maker
- • Colander/Pasta Strainer
- • Cooking Equipment
- • Cooking For Busy People
- • Cooking Thermometer
- • Corkscrew
- • Crockpot Recipes
- • Dessert
- • Diabetic Recipes
- • Dining Setup
- • Dip Recipes
- • Dutch Oven

- • Energy Bars
- • Food Preparation Equipment
- • Frying Pan/Skillet
- • Garlic Press
- • Gas Grill
- • Grass Fed Beef
- • Grater
- • Green Smoothie Recipe
- • Grill
- • Grilling Recipes
- • Healthy Cooking
- • Healthy Food Recipes
- • Healthy Recipes
- • Hot Sauce Recipes
- • How to Make a Burger
- • How to Make Kimchi
- • How To Make Hot Sauce
- • Indian Recipes
- • Induction Cooktop
- • Induction Stove
- • Japanese Chefs Knives
- • Japanese Food
- • Japanese Recipes
- • Japanese Sashimi
- • Japanese Sushi
- • Japanese Sushi Knives
- • Jerky Recipes
- • Kitchen
- • Kitchen Foil
- • Kitchen Scales
- • Kitchen Shears/Scissors
- • Kitchen Tool Organizer
- • Knife Sharpening/Honing Rod
- • Ladle

- • Lasagna Recipe
- • Marbling
- • Marquetry
- • Masher
- • Masonry
- • Measuring Cups
- • Measuring Jug
- • Measuring Spoons
- • Metabolic Cooking
- • Mexican Cooking
- • Mixing Bowl
- • Muffin Recipes
- • Oven
- • Oven Gloves
- • Oven Mitts
- • Ovenproof Dish
- • Paring Knife
- • Pasta Fork
- • Pizza Cutter
- • Plastic Containers
- • Plastic wrap/Clingfilm
- • Plastic Zipper Bags
- • Pork
- • Pork Recipes
- • Pots
- • Pot Holders
- • Raw Recipes
- • Restaurant Recipes
- • Restaurant Supplies
- • Roasting Tin
- • Rolling Pin
- • Run A Coffee Shop
- • Run A Restaurant
- • Salad Recipe

- • Saucepans
- • Seaweed Salad
- • Serving Equipment
- • Sieve
- • Slotted Spoon
- • Slow Cooker Recipes
- • Slow Cooking
- • Smoking Meat
- • Spatula
- • Stick Blender
- • Stirring Spoon
- • Storage Equipment
- • Sushi
- • Tea Towels
- • Thai Cooking
- • Tongs
- • Vegetable Peeler
- • Wheatgrass
- • Yam

11. Crafts and DIY

Crafts and DIY (Do-It-Yourself) encompasses a wide range of hobbies that people around the world are passionate about (and spend money on).

- • Airbrush
- • Balloon Animals
- • Bead Necklace
- • Beading
- • Beadwork
- • Build A Bunker
- • Build A Shed
- • Build A Surfboard

- • Build Container Home
- • Build Wood Burning Stove
- • Building A Chicken Coop
- • Building A Deck
- • Building A House
- • Building A Shed
- • Building Games
- • Cabin Plans
- • Cabinet Making
- • Calligraphy
- • Candle Making
- • Candle Making Supplies
- • Candle Molds
- • Card Making
- • Collage
- • Craft Supplies
- • Crochet
- • Crocheting
- • Cross-Stitch
- • Deck Plans
- • Decorative Candles
- • DIY Jewelry
- • DIY Solar Water Heaters
- • DIY Tutorials
- • Embossing
- • Embroidery
- • Engraving
- • Family Bunker Plans
- • Felting
- • Floral Design
- • Fretwork
- • Friendship Bracelet
- • Furniture Craft Plans
- • Glass Etching

- • Glass Making
- • Glass Mosaic
- • Glassware
- • Handmade Soap
- • Home Improvement
- • Home Improvement Loan
- • Homemade Gift Ideas
- • Homemade Jewelry
- • Homemade Soap
- • Homemade Soap Recipes
- • How To Build a Bar
- • How To Build a Boat
- • How To Build a Catapult
- • How To Build a Chicken Coop
- • How To Build a Deck
- • How To Build a Dog House
- • How To Build a Fence
- • How To Build a Fire Pit
- • How To Build a House
- • How To Build a Retaining Wall
- • How To Build a Shed
- • How To Burn Art
- • How To Make a Rug
- • How To Make Candles
- • How To Make Natural Cleaning Products
- • Kids Birthday Party Ideas
- • Kirigami
- • Kite Making
- • Knitting
- • Knitting Patterns
- • Lapidary
- • Learn Chainsaw Carving
- • Learn Food Carving
- • Learn How To Draw

- • Learn How To Paint
- • Learn Ice Carving
- • Leatherworking
- • Macrame
- • Make Your Own Jewelry
- • Model House Building
- • Model Ship Building
- • Model Sports Cars
- • Model Tank Building
- • Model Trains
- • Needlepoint
- • Needlework
- • Netting
- • Origami
- • Paper Craft
- • Paper Folding
- • Paper Making
- • Paper Toys
- • Papercraft
- • Patchwork
- • Porcelain Dolls
- • Pottery
- • Printmaking
- • Pyrography
- • Ribbon Embroidery
- • Sand Sculpting
- • Scrapbooking
- • Sewing
- • Shirt Printing
- • Silicone Soap Molds
- • Soap Making Recipes
- • Soap Making Supplies
- • Soap Mold
- • Soap Recipes

- • Stained Glass
- • Stamp Collecting
- • Stamping
- • Stickers
- • Stone Carving
- • String Art
- • Stuffed Toys
- • Sun Trellis Plans
- • Upholstery Supplies
- • Vegetable Carving
- • Weaving
- • Wholesale Candles
- • Wood Carving
- • Wood Framing Basics
- • Woodturning
- • Woodworking
- • Woodworking Plans

12. Diet and Weight Loss

Losing weight isn't just a necessity for many; it's also a passion and even a lifestyle. As a result, there are a ton of different diets and niches for you to choose from.

- • Acupuncture For Weight Loss
- • Advocare Diet
- • Alkaline Diet
- • Appetite Control Strategies
- • Apple Cider Vinegar Weight Loss
- • Apple Diet
- • Arthritis Diet
- • Atkins Diet
- • Ayurvedic Diet
- • Baby Food Diet
- • Balanced Diet

- • Banana Diet
- • Bee Pollen Diet
- • Best Weight Loss Pills
- • Best Weight Loss Program
- • Best Weight Loss Supplement
- • Beyonce Diet
- • Biggest Loser Diet
- • Bland Diet
- • Blood Type Diet
- • Boost Metabolism
- • Cabbage Diet
- • Cabbage Soup Diet
- • Calorie Intake To Lose Weight
- • Calories To Lose Weight
- • Candida Diet
- • Carb Free Diet
- • Cardiac Diet
- • Caveman Diet
- • Cayenne Pepper Diet
- • Celiac Disease Diet
- • Chia Seeds Weight Loss
- • Cholesterol Diet
- • Cleanse Diet
- • Clear Liquid Diet
- • Colitis Diet
- • Colon Cleanse Diet
- • Crohn's Diet
- • Dairy Free Diet
- • Dash Diet
- • Dash Diet Recipes
- • Detox Diet
- • Diet Direct
- • Diet Foods
- • Diet Meal Plans

- • Diet Pills
- • Diet Pills That Work
- • Diet Plans
- • Diet Plans For Women
- • Diet Recipes
- • Diet Shakes
- • Diet Tips
- • Dieting
- • Diets For Women
- • Diets That Work
- • Diets To Lose Weight Fast
- • Diverticulitis Diet
- • Dottie's Weight Loss
- • Dukan Diet
- • Easiest Way To Lose Weight
- • Easy Ways To Lose Weight
- • Eat Clean Diet
- • Elimination Diet
- • Extreme Weight Loss
- • Fast Diet
- • Fast Way To Lose Weight
- • Fast Weight Loss
- • Fast Weight Loss Diet
- • Fastest Way To Lose Weight
- • Fat Burners
- • Fat Burning
- • Fat Loss
- • Feingold Diet
- • Figure Weight Loss
- • Flat Belly Diet
- • Food Lovers Diet
- • Free Diet Plans
- • Free Weight Loss Programs
- • Fresh Diet

26

- • Fruit Diet
- • Gallbladder Diet
- • Gallstone Diet
- • Gaps Diet
- • Gastric Bypass Diet
- • Gastric Sleeve Diet
- • Gastritis Diet
- • Gastroparesis Diet
- • General Motors Diet
- • Gerd Diet
- • Gerson Diet
- • Gestational Diabetes Diet
- • Gluten Free Diet
- • Glycemic Index Diet
- • GM Diet
- • Gout Diet
- • Grapefruit Diet
- • Green Tea Diet
- • Green Tea Weight Loss
- • HCG Diet
- • Healthy Diet
- • Healthy Diet Plans
- • Healthy Diets
- • Healthy Weight Loss
- • Heart Healthy Diet
- • Herbalife Diet
- • Hiatal Hernia Diet
- • High Cholesterol Diet
- • High Fiber Diet
- • High Protein Diet
- • Hills Prescription Diet
- • Hollywood Diet
- • Hormone Diet
- • Hot Pepper Diet

- • How Can I Lose Weight
- • How Much Should I Weigh
- • How To Lose 10 Pounds
- • How To Lose 20 Pounds
- • How To Lose Belly Fat
- • How To Lose Belly Fat Fast
- • How To Lose Body Fat
- • How To Lose Weight
- • How To Lose Weight Fast
- • How To Lose Weight In A Week
- • How To Lose Weight Naturally
- • How To Lose Weight Quickly
- • Hypnosis For Weight Loss
- • Hypoglycemia Diet
- • Hypothyroidism Diet
- • I Need To Lose Weight
- • IBS Diet
- • Ideal Protein Diet
- • Ideal Weight
- • Inflammation Diet
- • Insulin Resistance Diet
- • Jennifer Hudson Weight Loss
- • Jillian Michaels Diet
- • Josh Peck Weight Loss
- • Juice Diet
- • Juice Diet Recipes
- • Juicing For Weight Loss
- • Keto Diet
- • Ketogenic Diet
- • Ketogenic Diet Menu
- • Ketosis Cookbook
- • Ketosis Diet
- • Kidney Detox
- • Kosher Diet

- • L Carnitine Weight Loss
- • LA Weight Loss
- • Lemon Detox Diet
- • Lemon Diet
- • Lemon Juice Diet
- • Lemonade Diet
- • Lemonade Diet Recipe
- • Liquid Diet
- • Liquid Diet Recipes
- • Lose 10 Pounds
- • Lose Love Handles
- • Lose Weight
- • Lose Weight Fast
- • Lose Weight Fast Diet
- • Lose Weight In 2 Weeks
- • Lose Weight In a Week
- • Losing Weight
- • Losing Weight Fast
- • Losing Weight Tips
- • Low Carb Diet
- • Low Carb Diet Plan
- • Low Cholesterol Diet
- • Low Fat Diets
- • Low Fiber Diet
- • Low Glycemic Diet
- • Low Iodine Diet
- • Low Oxalate Diet
- • Low Potassium Diet
- • Low Protein Diet
- • Low Purine Diet
- • Low Residue Diet
- • Low Sodium Diet
- • Low Sugar Diet
- • Macrobiotic Diet

- • Master Cleanse Diet
- • Medi Weight Loss
- • Medical Weight Loss
- • Mediterranean Diet
- • Mediterranean Diet Recipes
- • Metformin and Weight Loss
- • Metformin Weight Loss
- • Military Diet
- • Motivation To Lose Weight
- • New Diet Pill
- • No Carb Diet
- • No Sugar Diet
- • Oatmeal Diet
- • Paleo Diet
- • Paleo Diet Menu
- • Paleo Diet Recipes
- • Paleolithic Diet
- • Pancreatitis Diet
- • Pcos Diet
- • Pescatarian Diet
- • Plant Based Diet
- • Pre Diabetes Diet
- • Prescription Diet Pills
- • Prescription Weight Loss Pills
- • Primal Diet
- • Protein Shakes For Weight Loss
- • Quick Ways To Lose Weight
- • Quick Weight Loss
- • Quick Weight Loss Diets
- • Quickest Way To Lose Weight
- • Rapid Weight Loss
- • Raw Diet
- • Raw Food Diet
- • Renal Diet

- • Rice Diet
- • Scarsdale Diet
- • SCD Diet
- • Science Diet
- • Skinny Girl Diet
- • Slim Fast
- • Slim Fast Diet
- • Slow Carb Diet
- • Smoothie Diet
- • Smoothies For Weight Loss
- • Soup Diet
- • South Beach Diet
- • Special K Diet
- • Specific Carbohydrate Diet
- • Sugar Free Diet
- • Tapeworm Diet
- • The Dash Diet
- • The Fresh Diet
- • The Lemonade Diet
- • The Paleo Diet
- • The Zone Diet
- • Three Day Diet
- • Thyroid Diet
- • Tips To Lose Weight
- • TLC Diet
- • Tracy Anderson Diet
- • Ulcer Diet
- • Ulcerative Colitis Diet
- • Vegan
- • Vegan Diet
- • Vegan Diet Plan
- • Vegetarian Diet
- • Vinegar Diet
- • Vitamins For Weight Loss

- • Water Diet
- • Ways To Lose Weight
- • Ways To Lose Weight Fast
- • Weight Loss Blogs
- • Weight Loss Calculator
- • Weight Loss Challenge
- • Weight Loss Cleanse
- • Weight Loss Clinic
- • Weight Loss Diet
- • Weight Loss Foods
- • Weight Loss for Women
- • Weight Loss Meal Plans
- • Weight Loss Motivation
- • Weight Loss Pills
- • Weight Loss Pills For Women
- • Weight Loss Pills That Work
- • Weight Loss Plans
- • Weight Loss Programs
- • Weight Loss Recipes
- • Weight Loss Shakes
- • Weight Loss Smoothies
- • Weight Loss Stories
- • Weight Loss Success Stories
- • Weight Loss Supplements
- • Weight Loss Surgery
- • Weight Loss Tips
- • Weight Loss Workouts
- • Weight Watchers Diet
- • Weight Loss
- • What To Eat To Lose Weight
- • Wheat Free Diet
- • Yeast Free Diet
- • Yoga For Weight Loss

13. Digital Marketing and Making Money Online

Making supplemental income is a big priority for many, and the allure of doing it from the comfort of your own home is strong.

- • Affiliate Marketing
- • Amazon FBA
- • Amazon Selling
- • Blogging
- • Blogging For Money
- • Blogging Tips
- • Building Links
- • Drop Shipping
- • eBay Selling
- • Ecommerce
- • Email Marketing
- • Email Marketing Services
- • Email Marketing Software
- • Facebook Marketing
- • Google Ads
- • Google Ad-Sense
- • Google Shopping
- • Graphic Design
- • Extra Income
- • Internet Advertising
- • Niche Marketing
- • Online Marketing
- • Pay Per Click Advertising
- • Podcasting
- • SEO
- • SEO for Lawyers
- • Social Media Advertising

- • Social Media Marketing
- • Subscription Boxes
- • Video Marketing
- • Vlogging
- • Web Design
- • Web Traffic
- • Website Traffic
- • YouTube Channel

14.   Exercise and Fitness

The human desire to be liked and fit in, as well as the desire to achieve something, powers the latest exercise craze. There are hundreds of niches in this category that you can target to start your business.

- • Beach Body
- • Best Ab Workouts
- • Best Running Shoes
- • Best Workout
- • Best Yoga DVD
- • Best Yoga Mat
- • Biathlon
- • Bike Polo
- • Bodybuilding
- • Bodybuilding Diet
- • Bodybuilding Equipment
- • Bodybuilding Supplements
- • Bodyweight Workout
- • Body Detox
- • Building Muscle
- • Calisthenics
- • Cardio Exercises

- • Cardio for Moms
- • Creatine
- • Cross Country Running
- • Cross Country Skiing
- • CrossFit
- • CrossFit Exercises
- • CrossFit Games
- • CrossFit Shoes
- • CrossFit Workouts
- • Exercises To Lose Belly Fat
- • Exercises To Lose Weight
- • Fitness Coach
- • Fitness Motivation
- • Get A 6 Pack
- • Home Gym Equipment
- • Home Gym Equipment Ideas
- • How To Gain Weight
- • How To Gain Weight Fast
- • How to Walk Faster
- • How to Swim
- • Man Boobs
- • Military Training
- • Muscle Building
- • Muscle Building Diet
- • Muscle Pain
- • Personal Training
- • Personal Training for Seniors
- • Pre-Workout
- • Protein Bars
- • Protein Diet
- • Protein Diet Plan
- • Protein Shake Diet
- • Rowing
- • Running Gear

- • Running Holidays
- • Running Shoes
- • TRX Training
- • Tug of War
- • Walking
- • Weight Lifting
- • Weightlifting
- • Women's Fitness
- • Workout Routines
- • Yoga

15. Farming

As a response to the hectic and connected lifestyles of a modern office worker, there is a large community of people looking to go back to living off the land.

- • Agriculture
- • Ameraucana Chickens
- • Aquaponics
- • Baby Chickens
- • Baby Chicks
- • Backhoe
- • Baler
- • Bantam Chickens
- • Barn Plans
- • Chicken Breeds
- • Chicken Coop Designs
- • Chicken Coop Ideas
- • Chicken Coop Kits
- • Chicken Coop Plans
- • Chicken Coop Plans Free
- • Chicken Coops
- • Chicken Coops For Sale

- • Chicken Feed
- • Chicken Hatchery
- • Chicken Run
- • Chicken Tractor
- • Chicken Tractor Plans
- • Chicken Wire
- • Chickens For Sale
- • Chicks For Sale
- • Combine
- • Cult packer
- • Cultivator
- • Escardilla
- • Farming Equipment
- • Fix John Deere Tractors
- • Free Chicken Coop Plans
- • Greenhouse
- • Greenhouse Equipment
- • Greenhouse Farming
- • Greenhouse Plans
- • Greenhouse Supplies
- • Growing Tomatoes
- • Growing Your Own Food
- • Harrow
- • Harvester
- • Hatchery
- • Heritage Seeds
- • Hoe
- • Horse Breeding
- • Horseshoes
- • Horticulture
- • How to Grow Spinach
- • Hydroponics
- • Hydroponics System
- • Irrigation

- • Irrigation System
- • John Deere Lawn Tractors
- • Livestock
- • Machete
- • Manure Spreader
- • Motocultor
- • Peak
- • Plastic Mulch Layer
- • Plow
- • Plow Tractor
- • Raising Chickens
- • Raising Chickens For Eggs
- • Rake
- • Rhode Island Red Chickens
- • Seeder and Fertilizer
- • Shed Plans
- • Sheep Care
- • Shovel
- • Sickle
- • Sprayer
- • Sprinkler
- • Tractor
- • Transplanter
- • Wagon
- • What Do Chickens Eat
- • Wheelbarrow
- • Worm Farming

16. Fashion and Accessories

Clothes are no longer just something we use to stay warm; they are something we use to showcase our identity.

- • Analog Watches
- • Anklet

- • Ballroom Dresses
- • Bangle
- • Bathing Suits
- • Batik
- • Bespoke Clothes
- • Best Men's Watches
- • Big and Tall
- • Body Piercing
- • Bolo Tie
- • Bracelet
- • Brooch
- • Business Fashion For Men
- • Business Wear
- • Calendar and Moonphase Watches
- • Carcanet
- • Casual Watches
- • Cheongsam
- • Chiffon
- • Choker
- • Chronograph Watches
- • Chronometer Watches
- • Coats
- • Corsets
- • Cotton
- • Cowboy Boots
- • Cowboy Hats
- • Cufflinks
- • Day and Night Watches
- • Denim
- • Digital Watches
- • Dive Watches
- • Doublet
- • Dress Making
- • Dress Watches

- • Dresses
- • Ear Cuff
- • Earrings
- • Extra Large
- • Fascinator
- • Fashion Design
- • Field Watches
- • Flannel Shirts
- • Formal Wear
- • Formal Dress
- • Frock Coat
- • GMT Watches
- • Gospel Bracelet
- • Hairpin
- • Hatpin
- • Haute Couture
- • High End Fashion
- • Hybrid Watches
- • Islamic Clothing
- • Jewelry Appraisal
- • Jewelry Design
- • Jewelry Supplies
- • Kilt
- • Kimono
- • Kinetic Watches
- • Lithium-ion Watches
- • Luxury Brands
- • Luxury Watches
- • Mechanical Automatic Watches
- • Men's Suits
- • Men's Swimwear
- • Necklace
- • New Look
- • One Pieces

- • Organic Clothing
- • Pendant
- • Pilot Watches
- • Plaid shirts
- • Pleat
- • Plus Size
- • Preppy
- • Primal Wear
- • Quartz Watches
- • Rational Dress
- • Ring
- • Sarpech
- • Satin
- • School Uniform
- • Shirts
- • Silk
- • Skirts
- • Smart watches
- • Solar Powered Watches
- • Spring Drive Watches
- • Suits
- • Summer Dresses
- • T Shirts
- • Tailored Clothes
- • Tailored Suit
- • Thumb Ring
- • Tie-dye
- • Ties
- • Toe Ring
- • Tool Watches
- • Torc
- • Touch Screen Watches
- • Transfer
- • Tuck

- • Tuxedo rental
- • Tuxedos
- • Underwear
- • Uniforms
- • Velvet
- • Wool

17.   Fishing

Fishing isn't just a career for many. It's also a hobby with expensive equipment, with millions of passionate fishermen and women around the globe.

- • Bank Fishing
- • Bass Fishing
- • Boat Anglers
- • Bobbers
- • Bottom Fishing
- • Casting
- • Drift nets
- • Droplining
- • Fishing bait
- • Fishing boat
- • Fishing Equipment
- • Fishing Hook
- • Fishing Kayak
- • Fishing Knots
- • Fishing Line
- • Fishing Reel
- • Fishing Rod
- • Fishing Supplies
- • Fishing Tackle
- • Float Tubes
- • Fly Fishing

- • Ghost Nets
- • Gillnets
- • Hand Nets
- • Handlining
- • How To Drive A Fishing Boat
- • Ice Fishing
- • Jiggerpole
- • Jiggling
- • Kayak Fishing
- • Kite Fishing
- • Line Cutter
- • Longlining
- • Lures
- • Rock Fishing
- • Sinkers
- • Spearfishing
- • Sport Fishing
- • Surfcasting
- • Swivels
- • Tackle Box
- • Tangle Nets
- • Trawl Nets
- • Trolling
- • Trot lining
- • Trolling Motors for Sale

18.   Gardening and Lawn Care

A well-kept lawn and garden cannot just make a house more enjoyable, but more valuable. Because of this, millions of people invest their time and money into gardening and landscaping.

- • Backyard Chickens
- • Bad Boy Mowers

- • Bird House Plans
- • Bonsai Trees
- • Cheap Lawn Mowers
- • Composting
- • Conservation
- • Craftsman Lawn Mower
- • Craftsman Lawn Mower Parts
- • Craftsman Mower Parts
- • Craftsman Riding Mower
- • Dixie Chopper
- • Dixon Mowers
- • Edger
- • Electric Lawn Mower
- • Exmark Mowers
- • Fix Lawn Mower
- • Flower Seeds
- • Garden Fork
- • Garden Fountains
- • Garden Hoe
- • Garden Hose
- • Garden Knife
- • Garden Pests
- • Garden Scissors
- • Gardening
- • Gardening Equipment
- • Gardening Gloves
- • Gardening Tools
- • Grasshopper Mowers
- • Gravely Mowers
- • Growing Flowers
- • Growing Herbs
- • Hand Trowel
- • Herb Planting
- • Herb Plants

- • Honda Lawn Mowers
- • Honda Mowers
- • Husqvarna Lawn Mower
- • Husqvarna Mowers
- • Hustler Mowers
- • John Deere Lawn Mowers
- • John Deere Mowers
- • John Deere Riding Mowers
- • John Deere Zero Turn
- • Koi Fish Care
- • Koi Ponds
- • Kubota Mowers
- • Leaf Blower
- • Landscaping
- • Lawn Care
- • Lawn Mower Blades
- • Lawn Mower Parts
- • Lawn Mower Repair
- • Lawn Mower Reviews
- • Lawn Mower Tires
- • Lawn Mowers
- • Lawn Mowers For Sale
- • Lawn Tractor
- • Leaf Rake
- • Learn Tree Shaping
- • Loppers
- • Mowers Direct
- • Murray Lawn Mower
- • Murray Lawn Mower Parts
- • Permaculture
- • Plant Bulbs
- • Pruning Saw
- • Pruning Shears
- • Push Lawn Mower

- • Push Mower
- • Reel Mower
- • Riding Lawn Mowers
- • Riding Lawn Mowers For Sale
- • Riding Mowers
- • Scag Mowers
- • Self Propelled Lawn Mowers
- • Simplicity Mowers
- • Snapper Mowers
- • Snapper Riding Mower
- • Spade
- • String Trimmer
- • Toro Lawn Mower
- • Toro Lawn Mower Parts
- • Toro Lawn Mowers
- • Toro Mower Parts
- • Toro Mowers
- • Toro Zero Turn
- • Tree Planting
- • Troy Bilt Lawn Mower
- • Tulip Bulbs
- • Tulips
- • Urban Farming
- • Used Lawn Mowers
- • Vegetable Gardening
- • Vertical Gardening
- • Weeder
- • Zero Turn Mowers

19.   Health

Nothing is more important than health. It's a priority for every single human being. That's why there are hundreds of **niche** opportunities in this industry.

- • Acupuncture
- • Addiction
- • Adrenal Fatigue
- • Alcohol Addiction
- • Allergies
- • Allergy
- • Allergy Elimination Diet Plans
- • Allergy Supplements
- • Alternative Medicine
- • Amino Acids
- • Anal Bleeding
- • Anal Itching
- • Anal Pain
- • Anger Management
- • Angular Cheilitis
- • Ankylosing Spondylitis
- • Anorexia
- • Anorexia Nervosa
- • Aromatherapy
- • Arthritis Pain
- • Asperger's
- • Asthma Remedies
- • Asthma Treatment
- • Astigmatism
- • Autism
- • Back Pain
- • Bad Breath
- • Bad Habits
- • Best Eye Cream
- • Bipolar Disorder
- • Blood Pressure
- • Blood Sugar
- • Blood Testing

- • Blurry Vision
- • Brain Cancer Treatment
- • Brain Hacking
- • Brain Training
- • Breast Cancer Treatment
- • Bruxism
- • Bulimia
- • Cardiovascular Diseases
- • Cardiovascular Health
- • Child Obesity
- • Childhood Obesity
- • Colon Polyps
- • Constipation
- • Control Blood Sugar
- • Deafness
- • Dental Assistant
- • Dental Supplies
- • Depression
- • Detoxification
- • Diabetes
- • Diabetic Diet
- • Diabetic Diet Plan
- • Diet for Diabetics
- • Diet for Diverticulitis
- • Diarrhea Treatment
- • Drug Addiction
- • Drug Testing
- • Ear Infections
- • Eating Disorders
- • Eczema Treatment
- • Erectile Dysfunction
- • Erection Problems
- • Eye Diseases
- • Eye Exercises

- • Eye Floaters
- • Eye Health
- • Fatty Liver
- • Fatty Liver Diet
- • Fecal Incontinence
- • Fibromyalgia
- • Fibromyalgia Diet
- • Fire Safety
- • Fire Safety for Kids
- • First Aid
- • First Aid Training
- • Fissure
- • Fix Poor Posture
- • Floaters In The Eye
- • Flu Treatment
- • Foam Hand Grips
- • Food Addiction
- • Food Allergy
- • Genealogy
- • Genital Warts
- • Gingivitis Treatment
- • Glaucoma Symptoms
- • Glycemic Index
- • Gut Ache
- • Gynecomastia
- • Headache Relief
- • Health Care
- • Healthcare
- • Healthy Aging
- • Healthy Gut
- • Healthy Living
- • Healthy Snacks
- • Heart Attack
- • Herniated Disk

- • Hiccups
- • High Blood Pressure
- • Hip Pain
- • Hip Problems
- • Home Remedies
- • How to Get Smarter
- • How To Improve Eyesight
- • How to Improve Sleep
- • How To Live Longer
- • How to Whiten Teeth Naturally
- • How to Whiten Teeth with Baking Soda
- • Hypertension
- • IBS
- • Incontinence
- • Increase Growth Hormone
- • Increase Testosterone
- • Insomnia
- • Intarsia
- • Internet Addiction
- • Intraocular Pressure
- • Intrinsic Motivation
- • Irritable Bowel Syndrome
- • Itching
- • Jock Itch
- • Joint Pain
- • Lasik
- • Lasik Eye Surgery
- • Living Healthy
- • Low Self Esteem
- • Lower Back Pain
- • Lower Cholesterol
- • Lung Cancer Treatment
- • Massage Therapy
- • Masturbation Addiction

- • Medical Tourism
- • Menopause
- • Men's Health
- • Mental Health
- • Milk Allergy Treatment
- • Mobility Scooters
- • Mole Removal
- • Mood Swings
- • Mouth Ulcers
- • Nasal Polyps
- • Natural Cold Remedies
- • Natural Fever Remedies
- • Natural Healing
- • Natural Herbs
- • Natural Pain Relief
- • Natural Remedies
- • Naturopathy
- • Neck Pain
- • Nicotine Addiction
- • Nootropics
- • Nutrition
- • Obesity
- • Oil Pulling Teeth
- • Oral Health
- • Ostomy Supplies
- • Overweight
- • Pain Killers
- • Pain Relievers
- • Panic Attacks
- • Peanut Allergy
- • Personal Care
- • Piles
- • Polyphasic Sleep
- • Porn Addiction

- • Post Pregnancy Care
- • Premenstrual Syndrome
- • Prostate Cancer Treatment
- • Psoriasis
- • Psoriasis Diet
- • Quilting
- • Quit Smoking
- • Reflexology Treatment
- • Reiki
- • Restless Legs
- • Retinal Detachment
- • Rheumatoid Arthritis
- • Rheumatoid Arthritis Diet
- • Sinus Infection Treatment
- • Sinusitis
- • Sjogren's Syndrome
- • Skin Cancer
- • Sleep Disorders
- • Sleep Problems
- • Smartphone Addiction
- • Smoking Addiction
- • Smoking Cessation
- • Snoring
- • Stomach Pain Remedy
- • Stop Depression
- • Stop Loneliness
- • Stop Negative Thinking
- • Stop Overeating
- • Stop Snoring
- • Stress Management
- • Stress Relief
- • Stuttering
- • Supplements
- • Sweating

- • Tinnitus
- • Tooth Anatomy
- • Toothache
- • Trichotillomania
- • Varicose Veins
- • Vertigo
- • Video Game Addiction
- • Vision Therapy
- • Water Filter
- • Women's Health
- • Yeast Infection

20.   Makeup and Beauty

How people look affects first impressions, relationships, and even whether or not you get your dream job. No wonder there are countless beauty and makeup products to help people look their best.

- • All Natural Beauty
- • All Natural Makeup
- • BB Cream
- • Beard Care
- • Beauty Supplies
- • Beauty Tips
- • Blush
- • Blusher
- • Bronzer
- • Concealer
- • Contour Creams
- • Contour Powder
- • Dandruff
- • Dandruff Shampoo
- • Extension Eyelashes

- • Eye Primer
- • Eyebrow Gel
- • Eyebrow Pencils
- • Eyebrow Powder
- • Eyebrow Wax
- • Eyelash Adhesive
- • Eyelash Curler
- • Eyelash Glue
- • Face Powder
- • Face Primer
- • Fake Eyelashes
- • Foundation
- • Hair Care
- • Hair Loss
- • Hair Loss Cure
- • Hair Loss Treatment
- • Hair Regrowth
- • Head Lice
- • Highlight
- • How to Grow Hair Faster
- • Ingrown Hairs
- • Lip Balms
- • Lip Booster
- • Lip Gloss
- • Lip Liner
- • Lip Plumper
- • Lip Primers
- • Lip Stain
- • Lipsticks
- • Makeup Remover
- • Mascara
- • Men's Grooming
- • Men's Hairstyles
- • Nail Polish

- • Nail Polish Remover
- • Natural Makeup Remover
- • Organic Makeup
- • Rouge
- • Sensitive Scalp
- • Setting Powder
- • Setting Spray
- • Shampoo
- • Stubble
- • Teeth Whitening

21. Martial Arts

Martial arts is an important hobby for millions of children and adults alike. With expensive classes and equipment, there are plenty of niche opportunities available.

- • Age of Wushu Guide
- • Aikido
- • BJJ
- • Body Protector
- • Boxing
- • Boxing Gloves
- • Boxing Mitts
- • Boxing Shoes
- • Brazilian Jiu Jitsu
- • Contact Sticks
- • Focus Mitts
- • Freestanding Bag
- • Glove Deodorizer
- • Hand Targets
- • Hand Wraps
- • Hapkido

- • Headgear
- • Heavy Bag
- • Japanese Jujutsu
- • Jeet Kune Do
- • Judo
- • Karate
- • Karate Shoes
- • Kendo
- • Kenpo
- • Kick Shield
- • Kickboxing
- • Learn Arnis
- • Learn Bartitsu
- • Learn Capoeira
- • Learn Hapkido
- • Learn Kenpo
- • Learn Krav Maga
- • Learn Sambo
- • Learn Sanshou
- • Learn Savate
- • Learn Shooto
- • Learn Shotokan
- • Learn Silat
- • Learn Tai Chi
- • Mixed Martial Arts
- • MMA Equipment
- • MMA Gloves
- • MMA Training
- • Mouth Guard
- • Muay Thai
- • Muay Thai Pads
- • Neck Harness
- • Ninja Gear
- • Ninja Weapons

- • Ninjutsu
- • Qigong
- • Reflex Ball
- • Savate Shoes
- • Self Defense
- • Shaolin Kung Fu
- • Speed Bag
- • Steel Cup
- • Sumo Wrestling
- • Taekwondo
- • Teach Judo
- • Teach Karate
- • Urban Combatives
- • Wing Chun
- • Women's MMA
- • Wrestling
- • Wrestling Shoes
- • Wushu

22.   Music and Instruments

Music is another interesting intersection of passion, hobby, and career. There are plenty of opportunities to start a niche business in the music industry.

- • Acoustic Guitar Lessons
- • Acoustic Panels
- • Audio Interface
- • Banjo Lessons
- • Banjo Training
- • Bass
- • Bass Guitar Lessons
- • Bass Lessons
- • Bass Traps

- • Beat Maker App
- • Beat Making Tutorial
- • Choir Conductor
- • Condenser Mic
- • Conducting Music For Beginners
- • Control Surface
- • Diaphragm Condenser Microphone
- • Diffusers
- • Digital Audio Workstation
- • Direct Box
- • Dj Equipment
- • Dynamic Microphone
- • Electronic Drum Kit
- • Flute Lessons
- • Guitar
- • Guitar Lessons
- • Guitar Making
- • Headphone Amp
- • Headphones
- • How to Opera Sing
- • How To Rap
- • How to Rap Fast
- • How To Remember Lines
- • How to Scream Sing
- • How To Sing
- • How to Train Your Voice
- • Instrumental Bundles
- • Instrumentals
- • Learn To Play Guitar
- • Learn To Play Piano
- • Learn to Rap
- • Learn to Sign
- • Make Beats
- • Make Instrumentals

- • Microphone Preamp
- . Microphone Stands
- • Microphones
- • MIDI Controller
- • MIDI Keyboard
- • Monitor Isolation Pads
- • Monitor Management
- • Music Downloads
- • Music Players
- • Music Producing
- • Music Theory
- • Music Videos
- • Music Writing
- • Over-ear Headphones
- • Piano
- • Piano Lessons
- • Pop Filter
- • Power Conditioner
- • Rack Mount
- • Recorder Lessons
- • Reflection Filters
- • Sample Bundles
- • Samples
- • Singing Lessons
- • Snake Cable
- • Songwriting
- • Soundproofing
- • Studio Monitors
- • Studio Rental
- • Ukulele
- • Violin
- • Violin Lessons
- • Virtual Instruments

23.   Outdoors and Hiking

From hiking to bird watching and camping, there are a lot of outdoor activities that have their own niche.

- • Bear Hunting
- • Bird Watching
- • Boat Plans
- • Boating
- • Bow Hunting
- • Bow Mount Trolling Motor
- • Bowhunting
- • Camp Chairs
- • Camp Table
- • Campervan Travel
- • Camping
- • Camping Burners
- • Camping Equipment
- • Camping Pillows
- • Camping Stoves
- • Canoeing
- • Caving
- • Compass
- • Deer Hunting
- • DIY Buy Traps
- • Duck Hunting
- • Elk Hunting
- • Falconry
- • Flashlights
- • Fox Hunting
- • Guided Hiking Tours
- • Headlamps
- • Hiking
- • Hiking Gear

- • Hiking Guide
- • Hiking Maps
- • Hunting
- • Ice Climbing For Beginners
- • Jet Ski
- • Mountaineering
- • Outdoor Gear
- • Outdoor Wear
- • Propane Gas Cookers
- • River Rafting
- • Sailing
- • Single Burner Stoves
- • Sledding
- • Sleeping Bags
- • Sleeping Pads
- • Survival
- • Survival Kits
- • Survivalism
- • Survivalist
- • Tents
- • Trail Running Tips
- • Trapping
- • Trekking

24.   Pets and Animal Care

For many pet owners, their pets are part of their extended family. Keeping them healthy and happy is a priority they'll happily invest money in.

- • Aquarium Supplies
- • Aquatics
- • Bearded Dragon
- • Bearded Dragon Diet

- • Bulldog Care
- • Bulldogs
- • Fish Aquarium
- • Beekeeping
- • Beekeeping Supplies
- • Boxer Dogs
- • Cat Care
- • Cat Health
- • Cat Toys
- • Chinchillas
- • DIY Homemade Dog Food
- • Dog Apparel
- • Dog Backpacks
- • Dog Breeding For Beginners
- • Dog Friendly Hotels
- • Dog Grooming
- • Dog Health
- • Dog Potty Training
- • Dog Sledding
- • Dog Training
- • Exotic Pets
- • Ferret Care
- • Ferrets
- • Ferris Mowers
- • French Bulldogs
- • German Shepherd Care
- • German Shepherd
- • Healthy Dog Food
- • How To House Train A Dog
- • Micro Pigs
- • My Pet Chicken
- • Natural Dog Food
- • Pet Adoption
- • Pet Grooming

- • Pet Rehab
- • Pet Supplies
- • Pet Travel
- • Primal Dog Food
- • Puppy Care
- • Sick Cat
- • Sick Dog
- • Toilet Training

25. Sports

Not only are there a lot of different sports, there are also hundreds of different sports teams you can target with a niche site.

- • Air Guns
- • Air Hockey
- • Archery
- • Archery Supplies
- • Badminton
- • Base Jumping
- • Baseball
- • Baseball Jerseys
- • Basket Weaving
- • Basketball
- • Basketball Jerseys
- • Basketball Practice Plans
- • Beach Volleyball
- • Bike Racks
- • Bobsleigh
- • Bocce Ball
- • Bowling
- • Bouldering
- • Boomerang
- • Break Dancing

- • Bull Fighting
- • Capture the Flag
- • Cheerleading
- • Chess
- • Classical Dance
- • Cliff Diving
- • Cricket
- • Curling
- • Cycling
- • Cycling Gear
- • Cycling Holidays
- • Cycling News
- • Cycling Shoes
- • Darts
- • Decathlon
- • Dirt Bike Racing
- • Drone Racing
- • Equestrian
- • Esports
- • Fencing
- • Figure Skating
- • Fantasy Football
- • Fire Dancing Lessons
- • Flag Football
- • Foosball
- • Football
- • Football Jerseys
- • Football Betting
- • Football Trading
- • Free Climbing
- • Futsal
- • Golf
- • Golf Ball
- • Golf Carts

- • Golf Lessons
- • Golf Tips
- • Gymnastics
- • Handball
- • Hang Gliding
- • High Jump
- • Hockey
- • Hockey Jerseys
- • Horse Racing
- • How to Dive
- • How to Golf for Beginners
- • Ice Skating
- • Inline Skating
- • Inline Skating Tricks
- • Jai Alai
- • Jousting
- • Juggling
- • Jumpsuits
- • Kayaking
- • Kitesurfing
- • Lacrosse
- • Long Jump
- • Luge
- • Modern Dance
- • Modern Pentathlon
- • Motorcycle Racing
- • Mountain Biking
- • NASCAR Racing
- • Netball
- • Paddle Boarding 101
- • Paddle Boards
- • Paintball
- • Paintball Guns
- • Parachuting

- • Pilates
- • Pitching Machine
- • Piquet Strategies
- • Pole Dancing
- • Pole Vaulting
- • Quad Biking
- • Racquetball
- • Rafting
- • Rally
- • Rallying
- • Ringside Collectibles
- • Rock Climbing
- • Roller Skating
- • Rug Hooking
- • Rugby
- • Rugby Union
- • Shooting
- • Shot Put
- • Shuffleboard
- • Shuttlecock
- • Skateboarding
- • Skeet Shooting
- • Skydiving
- • Snooker
- • Snowboarding
- • Soccer
- • Soccer Betting
- • Softball
- • Spartan Race
- • Speed Skating
- • Spinner Bikes
- • Spinning
- • Sports Betting
- • Sports Massage Techniques

- • Sports Medicine
- • Sports Nutrition
- • Sports Tips
- • Surfing
- • Supercross
- • Swimming
- • Swimming Technique
- • Synchronized Swimming
- • Table Tennis
- • Tchoukball
- • Teach American Football
- • Teach Soccer
- • Teach Tennis
- • Teen Patti Strategies
- • Tennis
- • Tennis Holidays
- • Throwing Knives
- • Tour De France
- • Track and Field
- • Track Cycling
- • Trampolining
- • Triathlon
- • Volleyball
- • Wakeboarding Tricks
- • Water Polo
- • Water Skiing
- • Wheelchair Basketball
- • White Water Rafting
- • Windsurfing
- • Women's Golf

26. Technology and Gadgets

With desktop computers, laptops, mobile phones, and now smart watches, our society has become a lot more gadget focused.

- • 4K TV
- • Android Apps
- • Answering Machine
- • Anti Loss Alarm
- • Anti-virus Software
- • App Development
- • AR
- • Augmented Reality
- • Best Electronic Cigarette
- • Best Gaming Laptop
- • Best Juicer
- • Build A Computer
- • Build A PC
- • Building A Computer
- • Building A Gaming Pc
- • CB Antennas
- • CB Radios
- • Computer Monitors
- • Computer Programming
- • Computer Setup
- • CSS Tutorials
- • Drones
- • Ebook Reader
- • Electric Bikes
- • Electronic Book Reader
- • Electric Kettles
- • Ethernet Cable
- • Excel Tutorials
- • Fitbit
- • Game Console

- • Google Glass
- • Hoverboards
- • How To Build A Computer
- • How To Create Video Games
- • HTML Tutorials
- • Java Tutorials
- • JavaScript Tutorials
- • iOS Apps
- • IoT
- • iPhone
- • iPhone Apps
- • Jetpacks
- • Kindle
- • Laptop
- • Laser Printer
- • LCD Monitors
- • Learn C++
- • Learn JavaScript
- • Learn Php
- • Learn Python
- • Learning Html
- • Modem
- • Network Switch
- • Nintendo
- • Oculus Rift
- • Pager
- • PlayStation
- • Power Bank
- • PowerPoint Tutorials
- • Racing Drone
- • Retro Video Games
- • Smart Glasses
- • Smart Home
- • Smart Speaker

- • Smart TV
- • Smartphone Apps
- • Smart phones
- • Smart watch
- • Spyware Removal
- • TV
- • Television Set Up
- • Ultrabook
- • Universal Remote
- • Virtual Reality
- • Virtual Reality Headset
- • VR
- • Walkman
- • Wearable Tech
- • Wearable Technology
- • Word Tutorials
- • Xbox

27. Travel

The travel industry is full of different target markets and niches you can reach with a niche site or business.

- • Adventure Holidays
- • Adventure Tourism
- • African Safari
- • Backpacking
- • Backpacking on a Budget
- • Beautiful Places
- • Beautiful Scenery
- • Best Vacation Spots
- • Bungee Jumping
- • Cheap Airfare
- • Cheap Travel Tips

- • Couple Travelling
- • Cruise Travel
- • Cruises
- • Deep Sea Diving
- • Diving
- • Discount Travel
- • Family Trips
- • Family Vacation
- • Fear Of Flying
- • Finding Cheap Flights
- • Food Tourism
- • Gap Year Travel
- • Historic Travel
- • Last Minute Travel
- • Most Beautiful Places in the World
- • Places to Visit in New York
- • Route 66 Road Trip
- • Retirement Travel
- • Safaris
- • Sailing Holidays
- • Scuba Diving
- • Scuba Diving Holidays
- • Single Travel
- • Ski Holidays
- • Snorkeling
- • Stargazing
- • Staycations
- • Travel Luggage
- • Travel the World
- • Travel Tips
- • Trip To Vegas
- • Vacation Destinations
- • War Tourism
- • Wildlife Tourism

28. Wedding

As "the happiest day of our lives," most weddings are less concerned with frugality, and more with pomp and splendor. So there are several wedding niches with high earning potential.

- • Vintage Wedding Dress
- • Beach Weddings
- • Bridal Shower
- • Bridal Gown
- • Destination Wedding
- • Engagement Rings
- • Groomsmen Gift Ideas
- • Pear Shaped Engagement Rings
- • Wedding Advisors
- • Wedding Candles
- • Wedding Chapel
- • Wedding Dress
- • Wedding Gown
- • Wedding Party Dresses
- • Wedding Planner
- • Wedding Planning
- • Wedding Speech
- • Wedding Speeches
- • Wedding Supplies
- • Wedding Venues

400+ More Miscellaneous Potential Niches

The following niches don't fall under any of the major industries we've covered above. But that doesn't mean they don't have the same business potential.

- • Activities For Kids
- • Activities For Seniors
- • Affairs
- • Affirmations
- • Alternative Energy
- • Alternative Fuel
- • Amazon Shopping
- • Animation
- • Anti-Bullying
- • Antique Collecting
- • Antiques
- • Apocalypse Preparation
- • Arcade Machines
- • Artist Trading Cards
- • Assemblage
- • Astral Projections
- • Astrology
- • Auction Hunters
- • Auctions
- • Avoid Procrastination
- • Bachelor Party
- • Bachelorette Party
- • Backgammon Strategies
- • Bankruptcy
- • Battery Reconditioning
- • Be A Better Christian
- • Be A Better Jew
- • Be A Better Muslim
- • Be a Better Public Speaker
- • Be Successful
- • Beating Roulette

- • Bed Bugs
- • Bereavement
- • Best Anime
- • Best Dating Sites
- • Best Horror Movies
- • Best Movies Of All Time
- • Best Nursing Schools
- • Best Pick Up Lines
- • Best Stocks To Buy
- • Biker Dating
- • BioHacking
- • Biological Pond
- • Biometric Gun Safe
- • Birthday Party Ideas
- • Blackjack Strategies
- • Blenders
- • Board Game
- • Boarding
- • Body Tracking
- • Brain Teasers
- • Bridge For Beginners
- • Brighton Collectibles
- • Build Self Esteem
- • Bunkhouse Plans
- • Burglar Alarm
- • Burial Insurance
- • Busking
- • Card Tricks
- • Carpentry
- • Casino Bonus Offers
- • Celebrity Gossip
- • Chakra
- • Change Your Mind
- • Changing Bad Habits

- • Charades
- • Cheating Wife
- • Child Adoption
- • Child Custody
- • Child Modeling
- • Child Tutoring
- • Children Of Divorce
- • Children's Playhouse Plans
- • Christian Dating
- • Christian Marriage Advice
- • Christmas Gift Ideas
- • Cigar Smoking
- • Cigars
- • Classic Video Games
- • Cleaning Supplies
- • Closet Organizers
- • Coding
- • Coin Collecting
- • Coin Tricks
- • Colic
- • Commodity Investing
- • Conversational Hypnosis
- • Cool Math Games
- • Cosmic Energy
- • Cowboy Guns
- • CPC Exam Study
- • Credit Repair
- • Criminology
- • Cub Cadet Parts
- • Custom Bumper Stickers
- • Custom T-Shirts
- • Dacor
- • Dakota Collectibles
- • Dating After Divorce

- • Dating Asian Women
- • Dating Brazilian Women
- • Dating Latina Women
- • Dating Russian Women
- • Dating Thai Women
- • Dealing With Abuse
- • Death In The Family
- • Debt
- • Debt Consolidation
- • Decoupage
- • Derivatives
- • Disabled Dating
- • Distance Learning
- • Distraction
- • Divorce
- • Dollhouse
- • Dream Interpretation
- • E-Learning
- • EFT Tapping
- • Elearning
- • Electrician Training
- • Estate Planning
- • Event Hosting
- • Event Planner Certification
- • Event Planning
- • Excavation
- • Extrinsic Motivation
- • Female Pick Up
- • Final Expense Insurance
- • Forex
- • Forex Trading
- • Fundraising
- • Funeral Insurance
- • Gambling Addiction

- • Garage Sale
- • Geek Dating
- • Geocaching
- • Get Better Grades
- • Get Ex Back
- • Get Focused
- • Get Organized
- • Get Promoted
- • Goal-Setting
- • Going Green
- • Gold Mining Methods
- • Gold Panning
- • Gold Trading
- • Green Energy
- • Green Living
- • Green Power
- • Grieving Tips
- • Grow Taller
- • Gun Safety
- • Handgun Safety
- • Having Twins
- • Hearthstone Guide
- • Home Birthdays
- • Home Business
- • Home Cleaning
- • Home Energy
- • Home Laundry Detergent
- • Home Laundry Soap
- • Home Schooling
- • Home Security
- • Home Theaters
- • Homeschooling
- • Homesteading
- • House Floor Plans

- • House Pests
- • House Plans
- • House Restoration
- • House Sitting
- • How To Act
- • How To Be Famous
- • How To Be Happy
- • How To Be Rich
- • How to Be Smart
- • How To Build Credit
- • How To Build Confidence
- • How to Dress
- • How To Fight
- • How To Hula Dance
- • How To Hypnotize Someone
- • How To Increase Height
- • How to Make Friends
- • How To Pay Taxes
- • How to Speak Faster
- • How To Study Harder
- • Humanities
- • Hypnosis
- • Identity Theft
- • Identity Theft Protection
- • Iguana Care
- • Indian Dating
- • Internet Dating
- • Internet Safety for Kids
- • Interracial Dating
- • Islamic Marriage Advice
- • Janitorial Supplies
- • Jewish Dating
- • Jewish Marriage Advice
- • Job Interviews

- • Job Skills
- • Lansquenet Strategies
- • Latin Dance
- • Law of Attraction
- • Laying Laminate Flooring
- • League of Legends
- • Learn Arabic
- • Learn Basset
- • Learn Blackboard
- • Learn Body Language
- • Learn Braille
- • Learn Chemistry
- • Learn Chinese
- • Learn English
- • Learn French
- • Learn Latin
- • Learn Massage
- • Learn Maths
- • Learn Morse Code
- • Learn Russian
- • Learn Sign Language
- • Learn Spanish
- • Learn To Fly
- • Learning To Be Funny
- • Legal Advice
- • Legal Help
- • Lego
- • Lemon Laws
- • Lesson Plans
- • Life Coaching
- • Life Insurance
- • Living Will
- • Magic
- • Magic Tricks

- • Management Skills
- • Marine Biology
- • Marine Supplies
- • Marriage Help
- • Matched Betting
- • Medieval Collectibles
- • Medieval Games
- • Meditation
- • Mentalism
- • Midwifery
- • Millinery
- • Mind Setting
- • Miracle Brain System
- • Miracle Manifestation
- • Miracles
- • Mobile Technician
- • Monero Coin
- • Money Magnetism
- • Mortgage Refinance
- • Motivation quotes
- • Muskets
- • Mystery Shopping
- • Mystical Gods
- • Nail Biting
- • Nano Toys
- • Negotiation Skills
- • NLP
- • Numerology
- • Off The Grid Living
- • Off-road Racing
- • Office Depot Jobs
- • Office Supplies
- • Offshore Banking
- • Older Men For Younger Women

- • Online Bingo
- • Online Gambling
- • Online Games
- • Online Learning
- • Online Poker
- • Online Shopping
- • Online Sports Betting
- • Online Tutor
- • Palm Reading
- • Paralegal
- • Paralegal Schools
- • Paramedic Study Guide
- • Paranormal
- • Parenting
- • Parents
- • Parking Tickets
- • Party Decorations
- • Payday Loans
- • Penny Stocks
- • Pergola Plans
- • Personal Finance
- • Personal Loans
- • Petanque
- • Pick Up Artists
- • Pick Up Lines
- • Pilots Training
- • Pinball Machines
- • Pirate Ship Playhouse Plans
- • Plantar Fasciitis
- • Plastic Surgery
- • Play Poker
- • Police Training
- • Pool Supplies
- • Portable Charger

- • Power Tools
- • Power Walking
- • Powersports
- • Precious Stones
- • Private Investigation
- • Productivity
- • Psychic Powers
- • Pub Quiz Questions
- • Public Speaking
- • Radio Controlled Cars
- • Rc Cars
- • RC Planes
- • Real Estate
- • Real Estate Appraisal
- • Record Collecting
- • Record Label Business Plans
- • Recycling
- • Relationship Problems
- • Religion
- • Renovation
- • Reverse Mortgage
- • Reverse Phone Directory
- • Roman Weapons
- • Romance on a Budget
- • Romantic Ideas
- • Russian Dating
- • Save Marriage
- • Save Money At Supermarket
- • Save More Money
- • Save My Marriage
- • Saving For College
- • Saving Money
- • School Supplies
- • Screen Printing Supplies

- • Scrimshaw
- • Seduction
- • Segway
- • Self Help
- • Self Hypnosis
- • Sell Your Home
- • Selling Your Home
- • Senior Dating
- • Senior Living
- • Setting Goals
- • Sex Addiction
- • Sex Furniture
- • Shaky Hands
- • Shiatsu Massage Techniques
- • Shopping Addiction
- • Short Movies
- • Shyness
- • Sideshow Collectibles
- • Sign Language
- • Silent Movies
- • Single Parenting
- • Single Parents
- • Slots Machine Strategies
- • Social Anxiety
- • Solar Energy
- • Solar Power
- • Spas
- • Special Needs Children
- • Specialty Tea Lovers
- • Speed Dating Online
- • Spelling Bee Practice
- • Spiritual Healing
- • Spiritualism
- • Squash

- • Stand Up Comedy
- • Star Signs
- • Steam Trading Cards
- • Steampunk
- • Subliminal Messages
- • Success Habits
- • Surveys
- • Tapestry
- • Tarot Reading
- • Tatting
- • Tattoo Designs
- • Tattoo Removal
- • Tattoo Supplies
- • Tattoos
- • Tea Infuser
- • Tea Sets
- • Teacher Supplies
- • Team-Building
- • TEFL
- • Termite Control
- • Text Ex Back
- • Thai Massage
- • Theatre
- • Thought Elevators
- • Thrush
- • Time Management
- • Tiny Houses
- • Typography
- • UFOs
- • Visualization
- • Weird Science
- • Welding
- • Welding Supplies
- • Wind

- • Window Shopping
- • Window Stickers
- • Wireless Network
- • Witchcraft
- • Writing A Will